Combined Joint Task Force – Horn of Africa

Winning the War on Terror with Information Engagement

TABLE OF CONTENTS

INTRODUCTION

In the April of 1994, the plane carrying the presidents of Rwanda and Burundi exploded as it took off from the Kigali airport. This incident sparked a massacre that shocked the world with its scope and brutality. In three short weeks, with no international intervention, three to five hundred thousand Tutsi and moderate Hutu were killed, genocide on a scale not seen since WWII. By May, the Tutsi rebel army moved into the country and began to extract revenge upon the Hutu. The Hutu fled. NGOs operating in the region estimate that three hundred thousand Hutus fled east into Zaire. They were directed to an open volcanic plain north of Goma, Zaire by the local military.[3] It was when the suffering of these refugees gained international media attention that the U.S. deployed military forces to alleviate the humanitarian crisis. One of those units was an engineer company.[4]

In the thick darkness of the African night, a C-5 landed at Goma, Zaire [now the Republic of Congo]. The date was Friday, July 29, 1994 and on the aircraft was the first element of Army engineers deployed to Zaire as part of Operation Support Hope. When the sun rose that next morning the platoon leader and reconnaissance party traveled north from Goma on a narrow two-lane asphalt road to recon a proposed gravesite. The vehicle first passed poor locals then dry volcanic grassland and ultimately, about ten kilometers north of the airport, the refugees.

Although the NGOs in Goma called it a refugee camp, it was not recognizable as a camp. The term refugee camp implies an order and organization that was non-existent in this place. What was present was a mass of humanity stretching east from the road to the horizon extending north along the road for miles, thousands of campsites with minimal shelter. A haze of smoke trailed upwards from the few fire pits in which there was fuel for a fire. Lining the left or west side of the road were the bodies. Some long, some short, all rolled in a grass mat or blanket covering everything but the feet. It was on this side of the road she walked to the proposed gravesite.

---

[3]Samantha Power, *A Problem from Hell: America and the Age of Genocide* (New York: Perennial, 2003), 347-382

[4]The author was the platoon leader in this vignette. At the time she was the Earthmoving Platoon Leader in B/94th ECB(H), Vilseck, Germany.

Digging began the next day. When a reporter asked what it felt like to be digging graves on a Sunday, the platoon leader answered that she had not realized it was a Sunday. Probably it was that moment or shortly thereafter that the PA officer on site realized that the story would only get worse. The next interview would show U.S. soldiers operating bulldozers pushing bodies into the gravesite, possibly dismembering the bodies or crunching over bodies that slid under the blade. That next interview never happened. Conscious of the effect that a video of U.S. soldiers burying dead bodies would have on the American public, the command ended the platoon's mission once the hole was complete. Another organization filled the hole with bodies. The engineers moved on to construct roads at the site of a new refugee camp, approximately 40km north of Goma.

Road construction was the first step in constructing a true refugee camp. On the third or fourth day of construction, a SF Warrant Officer introduced himself to the platoon leader and told her the rebels would not attack her section. She thanked him and must have given him a puzzled look because he then went on to explain his comment. He was part of a Psychological Operations (PSYOP) team working in the area. In the course of his interactions he found out the rebels in the hills thought, we were constructing a military camp and were planning an attack. The engineers were completely unaware of this threat.

The construction of the camp, eventually named Kahindo, was the last project this detachment of engineers would complete in Africa. The Command had no desire to remain in country, "You're the long pole in my tent lieutenant," BG Nix stated, approximately 10 days into the deployment. The press camp adjacent to the military camp was dwindling and so was national interest. The last member of the engineer contingent departed Goma August 25, 1994, after less than four weeks on the ground.

Years later, as the platoon leader reflected on that mission to Africa, the hypocrisy of providing aid to the perpetrators of the genocide stood out like a neon sign. She better understood why the people in Africa might be suspicious of offers of U.S. assistance. Though the work done by the soldiers on the ground was an honest effort to provide life saving assistance to the refugees, their actions provided little support to the U.S. Government's strategic message because it was too late, in the wrong country and supported the population that had initiated the crisis. This was an example of an unsuccessful course of action at the operational and strategic levels. The tactical application of information engagement tasks was not sufficient to accomplish an operational or strategic victory.

Currently there is a task force operating in Africa that appears to have learned the lessons of when, where and who to support. Combined Joint Task Force –Horn of Africa (CJTF-HOA) focused on the Horn of Africa and neighboring countries since the fall of 2002. The success of CJTF-HOA supported the thesis that a course of action with information operations as the decisive operation is an adequate, feasible, and acceptable course of action to win the GWOT in regions such as the Horn of Africa. The CJTF-HOA course of action was successful in part because of the region therefore the discussion began with a description of the Horn of Africa. This formed the basis for why CENTCOM assigned a task force to the region and why the task force chose a course of action that emphasized information operations. Therefore, it is important to understand what information operations are.

Traditional military thinking focused on information operation tasks aimed at defeating the military forces of a near peer competitor, not an insurgent organization. To broaden that perspective, a summary of the theoretical concept of information operations led to a discussion of current Joint and Army doctrine. For ease of understanding, these concepts relate back to an example of a Medical Civil Action Project, a common mission in CJTF-HOA. The information concluded with emerging changes in Army doctrine. The changes identify and align staff responsibility for information operation tasks along war-fighting functions.

The next argument outlines the nature of a long war and the role of Information Operations in winning that type of war. The argument began by characterizing the current war as a long war. The U.S. declared war after the attack on September 11, 2001 and while there have been successful operations in the last six years; the end is not in sight. This is a long war, a war of ideas and it is therefore logical that information operations play a significant role.

In conclusion, CJTF HOA has had operational success with a course of action where IO is the decisive operation. The evidence proved the thesis that the chosen course of action was an adequate, feasible, acceptable course of action to achieve victory in the War on Terror. The success of CJTF-HOA and increased focus on information operations have led to doctrinal changes. The Army proposed reorganizing the IO capabilities along warfighting functions to facilitate planning and coordination of information operations. The conduct of information operations in CJTF-HOA and the doctrinal changes provide the basis for recommendations for future operations. The topics covered resources; command, control and coordination; and transition to civilian authority

CHAPTER 1 CJTF-HOA – A Strategy for Victory

Introduction

In October of 2002, the CENTCOM commander chose to open another front in the Global War on Terror, the Horn of Africa, and established Combined Joint Task Force – Horn of Africa (CJTF-HOA). The task force was to deny, defeat, diminish, and destroy terrorism in the region. The nature of the conflict in this region, the mission of the task force and the resources available to the task force led the command to choose a course of action with information operations (IO) as their decisive operation. The predominant IO task they conducted was Information Engagement. Because of the success Information Engagement has achieved, subsequent rotations have continued to emphasize Information Engagement.

Why the Horn of Africa?

Information Engagement is working in the Horn of Africa in a large part because of the nature of conflict in this area. The countries in the CJTF-HOA area of responsibility are Djibouti, Ethiopia, Eritrea, Kenya, Seychelles (islands east of Mombasa, Kenya), Somalia, Sudan, and Yemen.[5] This region spans over 5.2 million sq. km with a population approximately 165 million, almost 25%

---

[5]U.S. Department of Defense, CJTF-HOA, Public Affairs Office, "CJTF-HOA Fact Sheet." *CJTF-HOA Public Website.* (December 2006), 1. Refer to Annex A for a map of the Joint Operational Area.

of the entire population in Africa. It is a bridge between the Arabian Peninsula and the African continent.

The climate of the region varies between arid, desert lands along the coasts and Sahara Desert to forested mountain ranges with rivers and lakes in the interior. The region contains great cultural diversity and is composed of many nations, several that were recently at war with each other. The majority of the area lacks even the most basic infrastructure yet some urban areas have all the conveniences expected of a modern city.[6] Coffee is the main export of Ethiopia while trade and shipping generate most of the economic growth in the coastal nations.

Three nations in this region are key to resolving the conflict in the Horn of Africa. Ethiopia is strategically significant in the region because it has the third largest Muslim population in Africa, 33.65 million, larger than the Muslim population in Saudi Arabia, Sudan, Iraq, or Afghanistan.[7] The way in which Ethiopia governs its population and relates to its neighbors is an indicator of the direction of entire region, specifically the activity of Islamic fundamentalists in this region.[8] Kenya is a strategic center because of its long ties with the U.S. and attempts at Democratic government.[9]. Djibouti is important because of its location, at the point there the Red Sea open into the Arabian Gulf and important to the U.S. as a staging base for continued operations in the region. These three nations and their relations with the other nations in the region will shape the future of the Horn of Africa.

Successful GWOT operations have denied terrorists freedom to operate in areas they previously controlled. Intelligence and diplomatic cooperation between the U.S. and its allies made it much harder for terrorists to operate in First World countries. The U.S. liberation of Afghanistan and Iraq prevented Islamic Terrorist organizations from operating freely and openly without fear of persecution. Operations in Afghanistan specifically eliminated a key training ground. While web-

---

[6]R.D. Hermes, _____ Jebb, and _____ Hays, *Combined Joint Task Force - Horn of Africa Initial Impressions Report,* (Fort Leavenworth, Center for Army Lessons Learned, 2004), 40.

[7]The Central Intelligence Agency, "Ethiopia." *The World Factbook,* 2007.People.

[8]Sisay Asefa, "The Horn of Africa: Background, Scope and Regional Initiatives." *Addis Tribune* 30 May 03(World History Archives, Hartford Web Publishing, accessed 24 Jan 07), 5.

[9]Robert D. Kaplan, *Imperial Grunts : The American Military on the Ground,* (New York: Random House, 2005), 293.

based training is still available, a physical location provides sanctuary and sustainment required for extended operations. The terrorist groups may try to reestablish a sanctuary in a region of ungoverned or under-governed nation. A precondition in many under or ungoverned nations is regional conflict.

As illustrated in the opening vignette, the U.S. does not have a history of committed assistance on the African continent. Why is the region now significant enough to assign a dedicated Combined Joint Task Force and maintain it indefinitely? Author, political scientist, and Harvard professor Dr. Samuel P. Huntington provided some answers.[10] His theory proposed that post Cold War conflict would occur most frequently and violently along boundaries between cultures or civilizations rather than along boundaries separating political ideologies. Some may say he was prophetic in stating culture, not the state, would be the locus of future conflict.[11]

In his book, The Clash of Civilizations and the Remaking of World Order he argues that the "central and most dangerous dimension of the emerging global politics [is] the conflict between groups from different civilizations." Two of the seven civilizations he described are the Islamic civilization and Western civilization.[12] In addition to the conflict between these two civilizations in the Middle East, there is a simmering conflict occurring along the southwestern boundary of the Islamic civilization, in Africa. In the Horn of Africa, not only do Western and Islamic civilizations meet, but also they meet amidst many tribal cultures. The nature of these conflicts is cultural, ignited by politicization of ethnic differences.

One example is Sudan where a cultural and religious division has existed for many years between the northern Islamic states and the predominantly Christian states in the south. The northern Sudanese primarily live in large urban centers, while those in the south primarily subsist on a rural

---

[10]Dr. Huntington served as director of security planning for the NSC in the Carter administration and the international debate provoked by his 1993 article in *Foreign Affairs*, "Clash of Civilizations?" led to the publication of his book by the same name.
[11]Samuel Huntington, *The Clash of Civilizations and the Remaking of World Order,* (New York: Touchstone, 1997), 20,21.
[12]Huntington, *Clash of Civilizations,* 13,45,46.

economy. Sudan has considerable hydrocarbon resources and a large agricultural sector, though the country is one of the poorest in the world.[13] In Sudan, the government of Khartoum would lose 80% of its oil revenue if Southern Sudan votes to secede in 2011. More than the Islamic versus Christian division, the division of oil reserves between north and south motivate Khartoum to maintain control and delay resolution of this conflict.[14]

In addition to conflict and poverty, the Horn of Africa now faces the challenge of Islamic Fundamentalism or Political Islam on the rise. The Horn of Africa is a region where Christianity and Islam have co-existed for the last fourteen centuries.[15] The first significant action was the 1989 overthrow of Sudan's democratically elected government. The Iranian supported National Islamic Front claimed credit for this act. Another group that has recently threatened the Horn is the Al Ithaad al Islam (Unity of Islam). They have claimed responsibility for bombings and assassinations in Ethiopia.

One challenge in the region was the relatively weak state of the few nations who were following the path of democracy and the threat that fundamental religious organizations posed to the governments of those nations. The lack of the government's ability to provide for basic services or security created a vacuum that Islamic Fundamentalist organizations readily filled. There was an eightfold increase in the construction of mosques in the CJTF-HOA joint operational area. In addition, their teachings of fundamental Islam offered an ideological alternative to democracy that excited the young population and encouraged action.[16] With populations in diverse locations and repressed economies, providing equitable services to all people of the nation is a demanding task for the frail institutions of local governments.[17] To bolster these key nations in the region, CJTF-HOA

---

[13]U.S. Department of Energy. "Country Analysis Briefs- Horn of Africa." *Energy Information Administration, USG.* (February 2006), Sudan.
[14]John Prendergast, Colin Thomas-Jensen, "Blowing the Horn," *Foreign Affairs* Vol 86, No. 2 (March/April 2007), 72.
[15]Asefa, 1.
[16]Brian Michael Jenkins, Gregory F. Treverton, "Misjudging The Jihad: Briefing Osama on All the War's Wins and Losses," *San Francisco Chronicle*, (November 13, 2005).
[17]Kaplan, 293.

and the U.S. Department of State assisted the local governments in providing an alternative to Islamic Fundamentalists.

In summary, it is in this vulnerable region that the United States has established CJTF-HOA to take the offensive in the GWOT. The task force is operating in the Horn of Africa because of its location, the nature of the conflicts in the region and the need to deny terrorists a sanctuary. This was a preventative measure. The terrorist organizations would relocate from Iraq and Afghanistan to more isolated, ungoverned sanctuaries to continue their jihad. The U.S. strategy to deny these sanctuaries involves empowering the local governments and assisting them in their ability to provide for their people. The goal of this strategy is that the national governments are a preferred alternative to the Islamic Fundamentalist organizations.

Why Information Operations?

CJTF-HOA executed this strategy with a course of action that uses Information Engagement as the decisive operation. The factors that influenced the first rotation to select this course of action were the nature of the conflict in the region, their mission, and resources available to CJTF-HOA. The next three commands came to the same result, a course of action emphasizing Information Engagement. That fact reinforces the hypothesis that Information Engagement is an adequate, feasible, acceptable choice to win the GWOT in regions such as the Horn of Africa. In addition, for CJTF-HOA, winning the GWOT begins with the mission to win the War on Terror in the Horn of Africa.

The first CJTF-HOA rotation focused on detecting, disrupting, and ultimately defeating transnational terrorist groups operating in the region. Accomplishing this mission would deny the terrorists a safe haven in this area and diminish the support and material assistance from this region from enabling terrorist activity elsewhere. With this guidance, CJTF-HOA established as their mission the following statement. Counter the re-emergence of transnational terrorism in the region through civil-military operations and support of non-governmental organization operations with the goal of enhancing the long-term stability of the region. [18]

Their mission focused on preventing terrorism from gaining a foothold in the HOA. Intelligence indicated there were members of AQ and other terrorist organizations in the region but CJTF- HOA had little capability for direct action missions.[19] Though Special Operations teams had conducted targeted "snatch and kill" missions in the region, those missions were not the primary purpose of the task force. [20] Instead, the task force focused on gaining access to the nations in the Horn of Africa as well as the capability to influence the government officials.[21] The task force not only had to work with the host nations to accomplish this but the state department as well. The State Department was the lead agency for the Horn of Africa.[22] Because of this, the nature of the operations had to be palatable to the ambassadors and their staff to gain approval. This limited the type of operations that the task force could quickly execute.

The resources that CJTF-HOA had to accomplish this mission were also limited. Officers who had served in CJTF-HOA described the operation as an economy-of-force mission. According to them, it fell after Iraq and Afghanistan on both the DOD and CENTCOM's resourcing priorities.[23] The resources available to the task force included a headquarters location that was five months from completion, less than 1,500 personnel to include contract support, and whatever equipment was not needed in Iraq or Afghanistan.

At the beginning of the first rotation, the headquarters location was afloat. The first CJTF-HOA staff operated from the USS MOUNT WHITNEY for five months and then transitioned ashore

---

[18]Darric Knight, Lieutenant Colonel, U.S. Marine Corps. Email interview by author, 4 December 2006, Leavenworth. Transcript. Author in possession of transcript, Leavenworth, David P. Casey, Lieutenant Colonel, U.S. Marine Corps. Email interview by author, 6 December 2006, Leavenworth. Transcript. Author in possession of transcript, Leavenworth. Kilpatrick, Terrance G., Major, U.S. Army Reserve. Email interview by author, 18 December 2006, Leavenworth. Transcript. Author in possession of transcript, Leavenworth.
[19]Knight, Casey, Kilpatrick interviews.
[20]Kaplan,286.
[21]Knight, Casey, Kilpatrick interviews.
[22]Hermes, 33.
[23]Paul Warren, Lieutenant Colonel, U.S. Army. Email interview by author, 24 October 2006, Leavenworth. Transcript. Author in possession of transcript, Leavenworth.

to a former French Foreign Legion Fort, Camp Lemonier in Djibouti. It was difficult for the Commander and staff to travel and make the required coordination efforts with the host nations and U.S. embassies.[24] The easiest location for travel was Djibouti therefore the first missions focused on that country.[25] In addition to the challenge of a temporary headquarters, the rotation had few personnel to execute any mission.

CJTF-HOA grew from a marine expeditionary force (MEF) headquarters. The first rotation had two CA officers, one PA officer and a battalion of Marines assigned to the task force but no PSYOP personnel assigned. Two PSYOP LNOs from the CENTCOM headquarters in Qatar provided planning guidance and some products for the CJTF to use in the region. CJTF-HOA has an Area of Responsibility (AOR) five times larger Iraq and Afghanistan combined and less than 1,500 military, government and contract personnel to execute their mission. Even that number is misleading in terms of operational capability. The majority of those personnel support operations from Camp Lemonier. Even at its peak, less than two hundred personnel were conducting operations outside Djibouti. Subsequent rotations received a civil affairs company and a psychological operation team. Clearly, the task force would have to accomplish their mission with minimal use of U.S. military personnel.[26]

The nature of their mission, the headquarters infrastructure, and personnel available to conduct operations in this region influenced the first rotation's course of action selection. Gaining entry to a country was critical to mission accomplishment therefore the planning group recommended and the commander approved a course of action in which Information Engagement was the decisive operation.[27]

The IO task of Information Engagement utilized the information operation capabilities of Public Affairs (PA), Psychological Operations (PSYOP), and Combat Camera (COCAM) in

---

[24]Hermes, 35.
[25] Knight, Casey, Kilpatrick interviews.
[26]Hermes, 1.
[27]Knight, Casey, Kilpatrick interviews.

coordination with Civil Affairs (CA) and Defense Support to Public Diplomacy (DSPD).[28] Because

the CA and DSPD missions were conducted in coordination with and in support of CJTF-HOA's

mission, they were categorized as parts of the Information Engagement task. The medical and

veterinary visits to the region were examples of Civil Military Operations coordinated by the Civil

Affairs teams. The mil-to-mil training events that CJTF-HOA conducted were examples of DSPD.

The first rotation successfully accomplished their mission with this course of action. In its first three

years, the task force "renovated 33 schools, eight clinics, and five hospitals; dug 11 wells; and

conducted nearly 40 medical and veterinary visits."[29]

The success of the information operations course of action chosen in those first three years

may have persuaded BG Robeson to maintain that course of action. It may have been that the same

factors that influenced the course of action chosen by the first CJTF-HOA rotation, the nature of the

conflict in the region, their mission, and resources available to CJTF-HOA led him to choose a course

of action emphasizing Information Engagement. The new rotation continued to plan missions to gain

entry and access to areas while projecting a positive image of the United States in the region.

MG Ghormley, who succeeded BG Robeson, also chose a course of action that centered on

Information Engagement. In a news briefing in 2005 he explained that the task force conducted CMO

and training missions (TSC) to "combat terrorism, and to establish a secure environment and regional

stability. You cannot have any type of peace, you cannot have any type of prosperity without security

and stability, and that is our goal.[30] The current CJTF-HOA rotation under the command of Admiral

Hunt has continued this trend.

The missions conducted by CJTF-HOA started small but have made a steady impact in these

three nations and the region. Through three different commands, CJTF-HOA's course of action

---

[28]Hugh Rogers, "FM 3-0 Issue Paper: Information Operations (IO)," 5 pages, (FOUO) Combined Arms Doctrine Directorate, U.S. Army Combined Arms Center (February 2007) 3.
[29]CJTF-HOA PAO, "CJTF-HOA Fact Sheet," 1.

[30]Maj. Gen. Timothy Ghormley, "News Briefing with Maj. Gen. Timothy Ghormley." *U.S. Department of Defense* . 21 September 2005. (Office of the Assistant Secretary of Defense (Public Affairs), 3

continued with Information Engagement as the decisive operation and has produced positive results. However, as illustrated by the vignette in the first pages of this document, successful information operations are not an automatic result of executing Information Engagement or any other IO task. Despite the fact that the Public Affairs, Psychological Operations and Engineer (supporting the civil military operations) units all participated in Operation Support Hope, the operation was a failure from the IO perspective. So what criteria will prove that CJTF-HOA is conducting a successful operation?

CJTF-HOA – Achieving Victory

CJTF-HOA is a joint operation so the joint evaluation criteria will serve as the basis to assess the validity of the campaign as a COA to win the GWOT. Joint Military doctrine states that a valid COA is one that is adequate, feasible, acceptable, distinguishable, and complete.[31] Since the CJTF-HOA commander has already chosen a course of action, the following analysis is limited to the remaining criteria, adequate, feasible, and acceptable. The discussion will begin with the doctrinal definition of the criteria primarily focusing on Joint Doctrine and proceed with examples of CJTF-HOA missions that support success in those criteria, beginning with adequacy.

As defined in joint doctrine, adequacy predicts whether the scope and concept of planned operations can accomplish the assigned mission and comply with the planning guidance provided.[32] Army doctrine uses the word suitable but the definitions are similar.[33] The mission and planning guidance for each CJTF-HOA rotation were similar. While the exact mission statements have varied slightly, every one had at its core, the 4D Strategy, defeat, deny, diminish, and defend. The task force was to defeat the terrorists and their organizations in the Horn of Africa, deny terrorists sponsorship,

---

[31]U.S. Department of Defense, Director for Operational Plans and Interoperability (J-7), *Joint Publication 5-0, Joint Operation Planning* (Washington, DC: Joint Staff, 2006), III-24

[32]U.S. Department of Defense, Director for Operational Plans and Interoperability (J-7), *JP 5-0* GL-4

[33]**Suitable**. A COA must accomplish the mission and comply with the commander's planning guidance. U.S. Army Doctrine Proponency Division, *Field Manual 5-0, Army Planning and Orders Production* (Fort Leavenworth: US Army Combined Arms Center, 2005), 3-29

support, and sanctuary in the region, diminish the conditions that terrorists can exploit, and defend U.S. national interests in the region.[34]

The planning guidance was minimal but it included the fact that CJTF-HOA was third in the CENTCOM priority[35]. The examples illustrate the adequacy of an economy-of-force mission. What the planning guidance did not say was also relevant to the adequacy of the COA. Nowhere in the planning guidance for any of the four rotations to date was there a date to end operations, to pull out. This freedom has encouraged the leaders in the task force to take a generational approach with their COA. More than one senior leader in CJTF-HOA has described this mission as one requiring generations to take hold and truly bear out the success of the Information Operations.[36]

Measures of effectiveness assess the adequacy of the chosen COA, specifically the success of a mission or operation in accomplishing its intended goal.[37] The examples from CJTF-HOA have few quantifiable measures of success. It is hard to gauge the measures of effectiveness of a CA project, yet some measurement is required. Many of the effects will manifest themselves in the long term, so they are not easily identifiable. However, some measures that indicate short-term progress. For example, if the number of requests for projects increases, then it is a good sign that the host nation is pleased. This gives the task force continued access to that nation and the opportunity to expand its access.

Another measure, according to a report from the Center for Army Lessons Learned, is the "non-CNN" effect. In other words, a lack of activity in an area around the CA project may indicate

---

[34]U.S. National Security Council, *The National Strategy for Combating Terrorism*, (Washington, DC: White House, 2003), 15-24.

[35] Knight, Casey, Kilpatrick interview 2006.

[36] Comment made by MG Ghormley "And it's a generational perspective. And of course, generational means a long time. We're not there for a few years. It took forever for the terrorists to finally percolate to the top, and it's going to take just about as long to get them to go back down again. At some point, those nations that have asked for our help will be able to stand on their own, be able to thank us, and we'll know it's time to go home." And a similar comment made by COL Huddleston in his SITREP #3.

[37]**measure of effectiveness**. A criterion used to assess changes in system behavior or capability that is tied to measuring the attainment of an end state, achievement of an objective, or creation of an effect. U.S. Department of Defense, Director for Operations (J-3) *Joint Publication 3-0, Joint Operations* (Washington, DC: Joint Staff, 2006), GL-22.

the building of good will. The importance of good will is that it offers an alternative to extremist ideology, so signs of good will are indicators that the CJTF is fighting the extremists with tangible actions.

Many of the CA projects have bolstered the host nation government's legitimacy. These projects support the overall plan and include school construction, road construction, well digging, inoculation programs, de-worming livestock programs, and individual treatment of ailments. These activities, again, develop goodwill and bring legitimacy to the government in areas challenged by extremism that is challenging government legitimacy. These projects also offer people tangible evidence of US good will that challenges extremist ideology. Many people in the area are undecided about the US, so taking advantage of this opportunity to provide concrete steps towards increasing quality of life and even survivability helps counter extremist ideology..

> "The people of Qabridahar welcome the U.S. Army's Civil Affairs Unit. [It is very] tough to claim any type of objective success. I can't tell you that I have a bag of hearts and a bag of minds here -- you know, 17 hearts, 12 minds, these are mine -- because one, you just can't do it; and two, you could lose it the next day. But when you're welcomed back on a continuing basis and they're excited to see you, when you leave they are asking you to come back, there is a measure of effectiveness."[38] Maj. Gen. Timothy Ghormley to Reporters in a News Briefing 21 Sep 2005

The command can measure some effects quantitatively. One of the many successes of the unit has been its program that treated approximately 25,000 animals. Another medical program treated approximately 1,500 patients. "People traveled great distances to participate...again a good sign."[39]

Throughout the four plus years that CJTF-HOA has been in operation, the task force has accomplished much. Since CENTCOM established CJTF-HOA, there has not been one terrorist attack in the Horn of Africa, although there have been attempts.[40] A significant measure of

---

[38]Ghormley, "News Briefing ," 5.
[39]Hermes, 8.
[40] CJTF-HOA PAO, "CJTF-HOA Fact Sheet," 1.

effectiveness is the level of host nation capacity to ensure its own security and that it views its own security with a regional perspective.

The task force has trained military forces in Kenya, Djibouti, Tanzania, Uganda, Ethiopia, and Yemen. In the winter of 2004, Yemeni forces trained by U.S. Marines captured dozens of al-Qaeda suspects.[41] Ethiopia's intervention into Somalia January of 2007 not only demonstrates the nation's capability to defend itself against the radical Islamic threat but the determination to defeat that threat before it entered Ethiopia. This local capacity is the goal of the GWOT[42]. The key for CJTF-HOA in accomplishing this goal was to gain access and establish a presence. Although responsible for seven nations, CJTF-HOA initially had access to only three. .[43] The CJTF now has teams operating in six countries [44]

In summary, the COA that CJTF-HOA is pursuing is adequate. The examples illustrate the task force has defeated terrorists or radical Islamists in Yemen, Djibouti and Somalia The lack of attacks since the task force arrived is a positive indication that CJTF- HOA is denying the terrorists the freedom to operate in that region. The Civil Military Operations (CMO) have diminished the conditions the terrorists exploit. In addition, the mil-to-mil training builds capable partners in the GWOT to aid U.S. forces in defending U.S. interests. The next evaluation reviews the feasibility of the course of action.

Feasibility predicts whether the assigned mission can be accomplished using available resources within the period contemplated by the plan.[45] When the leadership of CJTF-HOA comments on the timeframe of the mission, they speak of generations. CJTF-HOA is planning for a long war. Timeframes that may not be "contemplated by the plan" are the political timeframe and popular timeframe. The 2006 election results, which gave Democrats a majority in both houses of

---

[41]Kaplan, 287.
[42]U.S. National Security Council, *The National Strategy for Combating Terrorism*, (Washington, DC: White House, 2003), 30.
[43]Hermes, 9,15.
[44]CJTF-HOA PAO, "CJTF-HOA Fact Sheet," 1.
[45]U.S. Department of Defense, Director for Operational Plans and Interoperability (J-7), *JP 5-0* GL-11.

Congress, and subsequent attempts to tie the budget for the war to a timeline, indicate that operations in both Iraq and Afghanistan are up against those timeframes.

Available resources in the case of CJTF-HOA are those resources allocated to CENTCOM and not committed to Iraq or Afghanistan. As shown in the previous section, resources available to date have accomplished the mission. An example of the effect a small detachment of soldiers can have is in the town of Yoboki in Djibouti. The project lasted five months but upon its completion, that town of 1,500 people will have fresh water for the next 10 years.[46].

Investing time and resources to coordinate with embassies has also helped CJTF-HOA accomplish its mission. To deploy CJTF forces into any country requires country clearance. In some cases, this takes as long as two weeks. Then the task force created country coordination elements (CCE) to work in the embassies with the State Department. The CCE provide that personal contact and service which reduced the processing time for country clearances to less than a week. This improved efficiency was worth the loss of the staff members to the CJTF. The CCE has now expanded its role to facilitate CMO project approval.[47]

In addition to adding the country coordination elements to the embassies, the joint operations center has designated country desk officers in the J-3 and country plans officers in the J-5. This provides continuity in planning and executing missions in each of the nine countries in the JOA. With these changes, the military has shown the ability to adjust its doctrinal C2 structure to facilitate interagency coordination.[48] This has set a precedent not only for future operations in CJTF-HOA but for future operations in other areas of the world where the military and the State Department together are fighting the GWOT.

The CMO effort is the centerpiece of the task force. From the first rotation, CMO provided access and presence, which were critical to the task force succeeding in its mission. The commander

---

[46]Ghormley, "News Briefing ," 3.
[47]Hermes, 114.
[48]Hermes, 114.

of the first rotation viewed CMO as a method to shape the battle space and create favorable conditions that will encourage stability and offer an alternative to extremist ideology.[49] The staff vetted all CA projects to verify they supported the overall purpose of the operation. The key was to gain access and establish presence. CA integration was a multifaceted effort that included not only integration among the staff elements of the task force, but also among the various interagency and host nation players.[50]

In summary, operations in CJTF-HOA are feasible because they have adequately accomplished the mission with the resources available and within the currently planned timeframe. All commanders have viewed this operation from a generational approach that is consistent with the requirements of a long war. The task force has developed partners, not only with other nations but also with the U.S. State Department officials in the region. In addition, as the amount of resources needed in other regions of CENTCOM or the greater GWOT decline, CJTF-HOA may have access to more resources to continue its success. The final assessment criterion is acceptability.

As defined in the glossary of the 2006 version of JP 5-0, Joint Operation Planning, acceptability is the determination as to whether the contemplated course of action is proportional and worth the cost in labor, materiel, and time involved; is consistent with the law of war; and is militarily and politically supportable.[51] Unlike a major combat invasion of a hostile nation where the host nation does not get a vote on whether the COA is acceptable, the COA used in CJTF-HOA must be acceptable to the host nation as well as the United States. One piece of evidence supporting the acceptability of this COA is that CJTF-HOA has successfully influenced the countries of Ethiopia, Djibouti, Yemen, Eritrea, Kenya, and the Seychelles, to collaborate with the U.S. in the GWOT.[52]

Maintaining good relations with the Kenyan military allows the U.S. to provide financial support to the Kenyan military and thus government, and reap the benefit of those improvements that

---

[49]Knight, Casey, Kilpatrick interview 2006.
[50]Hermes, 7.
[51]U.S. Department of Defense, Director for Operational Plans and Interoperability (J-7), *JP 5-0* GL-4.
[52]CJTF-HOA PAO, "CJTF-HOA Fact Sheet," 1.

support U.S. operations. One example is a joint American Kenyan exercise, Edged Mallet, which

takes place near Kenya's northern coastal border with Somalia.[53] Manda Bay is the base for the

exercise. It is a Kenyan air base and naval station, both of which received needed upgrades to better

support the exercise. The improvements help the military and through them, the government of

Kenya, maintain the security of its border security. The benefit to the U.S. military is the ability to

keep CA teams in Manda Bay to maintain good relations with the civilian community and, through

those relationships, gain intelligence to fight the GWOT. .[54]

Acceptability of a COA to the international community is also a consideration. In a news

briefing, MG Ghormley stated,

> "We've been working with the Kenyan Coast Guard as well
> as with the Yemeni Coast Guard. We had an officer stand up the
> Yemeni Coast Guard over a two-year [period]. [When the] U.S.
> Coast Guard officer moved on. The U.K. moved in and then picked
> up right where we left off. We've been having a great partnership
> with our British brethren working on our mil-to-mil as well as some
> of our CA projects."[55]

This course of action has also been acceptable to France, a full partner in the U.S. efforts in

CJTF-HOA.

CJTF-HOA has achieved small victories in their regional war on terrorism. The military plan

supports the generational timeline necessary to win a long war. In general, the press coverage and

political statements concerning military operations in the Horn of Africa have been positive.

Operations in Somalia to remove the Islamic government have drawn criticism of government

policies and actions but author made no disparaging accusation specifically directed at CJTF-HOA.[56]

However, some Western diplomats and experts warned that U.S. policy in the Horn of Africa might

be making it easier for al-Qaeda to gain a foothold in the strategic region, the noticeable lack of

---

[53]Kaplan, 293.
[54]Ibid., 294.
[55]Ghormley, "News Briefing, " 6.
[56] Steve Mbogo, "U.S. Horn of Africa Task Force Steps up Operations." *World Politics Watch – A Foreign Policy and National Security Daily* , 9 August 2006, 1.

terrorist activity counters that opinion.[57] Despite the criticism, most reports on the operations of CJTF-HOA have been positive. This is an indication of success in the GWOT. Future commands do have to be prepared for more national and international scrutiny from the press as operations in Iraq and Afghanistan wane and be aware that negative public opinion has the ability to shorten the military timeline.

MG Ghormley's emphasis on the participation of the host nation underscores one of the many successes that have come from this course of action emphasizing Information Engagement. This and the other successes described illustrate that this course of action was an adequate, feasible, and acceptable course of action to win the War on Terror in the Horn of Africa. The scope and concept of the operation has accomplished the assigned mission and complied with the planning guidance provided. CJTF-HOA has accomplished their mission within their resource constraints and done it in an acceptable manner. The course of action was acceptable to the State Department, to the American politicians and public and most importantly, to the people and governments in the region. Meeting these criteria, especially acceptability, increases the likelihood that the task force will remain until the local governments achieve the capacity to win the War on Terror themselves.

Conclusion

The sustained presence of Combined Joint Task Force - Horn of Africa in the region is evidence that, at least in this case, the U. S. has learned from its performance in Operation Support Hope. The Soldiers, Sailors, Airmen and Marines can look back on their service and see proof that their efforts at the tactical level resulted in operational and, potentially, strategic victories in the Global War on Terror.

Because of its population, location, and potential resources the Horn of Africa is strategically important to the United States. The region has approximately twenty-five percent of the entire

---

[57]John Prendergast, Colin Thomas-Jensen, "Blowing the Horn," *Foreign Affairs*, Vol. 86, No. 2, (March/April 2007) 59. and CJTF-HOA PAO, "CJTF-HOA Fact Sheet," 1.

population in Africa and continues to grow. Arab and African Muslims are a significant percent of not just the African population but of the world Muslim population. There are more Muslims in Ethiopia than there are in Saudi Arabia, Iraq, or Afghanistan. This population is key terrain in the Global War on Terror.

The region was important because of its physical terrain as well. The region's location, on the southern border of the historic Caliphate, increased the potential for a Clash of Cultures. This clash was responsible for the difficulty in governing the nations in the region. Nations that had areas that were ungoverned or under-governed attracted terrorist organizations. The terrorists sought sanctuary from the U.S. and other nations fighting the GWOT in these ungoverned or under-governed regions.

These regions provided terrorists with resources in addition to sanctuary. These resources were in the form of money, recruits, or supplies. In the case of Sudan, much of the money came from the oil wealth controlled by the government in the north. CJTF-HOA operations have uncovered terrorist recruits in Kenya and Somalia. The many armed conflicts in the region also provided a steady supply of weapons. This provided the terrorist organizations easy access to large quantities of arms and ammunition. This chaos also made it difficult for the U.S. to prove that nation states outside the region supplied terrorist organizations.

Despite these challenges, CJTF-HOA developed a course of action to win the War on Terror in the Horn of Africa. Because of the mission, resources available to the task force, and the nature of the conflict, the command chose a course of action that used Information Operations as the decisive operation. Specifically they focused on the Information Operation task of Information Engagement to accomplish the mission.

The mission of the task force was broad – defend, deter, diminish, and ultimately defeat terrorists in the region. The region in which CJTF-HOA had to execute this mission included six nations and one failed state. The area was larger than Iraq and Afghanistan combined. Those first planners also knew that the task force would have to accomplish this mission in a way that would support CENTCOM and the U.S. mission to win the Global War on Terror in the rest of the world.

The resources available to the planners to accomplish this mission were 1,500 Soldiers, Sailors, Airman, and Marines. The requirements in Afghanistan and later, Iraq limited their access to equipment and personnel not organic to the task force. Therefore, the planners recommended a course of action that maximized the contribution of the Civil Affairs and Public Affairs officers, combat camera, no more than a battalion of Marines, and the Medical, Veterinary and Engineer units that rotated through the region. Later rotations had a PSYOP team assigned to the task force but the first rotations relied on limited support from two PSYOP LNOs from CENTCOM.

The other factor that limited the courses of action available to the task fore was the nature of the conflict. It was not armed conflict with a peer competitor. This was a struggle of ideas where rivals competed for the support of the population. The nature of this conflict imposed a set of rules on the task force. Unless their target was a known or suspected international terrorist, CJTF-HOA had to operate with the permission of the host nation. Entering the host nation required a country clearance. This meant the task force needed the permission of the U.S. State Department. In addition, for civic action projects like MEDCAPS or VETCAPS, the task force needed to have the approval of the local population.

Despite this "soft" approach, CJTF-HOA was not the Peace Corps. Their operations had to accomplish their mission. The course of action that accomplished their mission with the resources available was one in which Information Operations was the decisive operation, specifically the task of Information Engagement. This approach used the resources of the task force to influence the local populations, host nation governments, and international partners to join CJTF-HOA in fighting the Global War on Terror. Subsequent rotations continued with this course of action and have succeeded in winning the Global War on Terror in the Horn of Africa. The accomplishments of CJTF-HOA measured against the U.S. Military Joint Doctrinal criteria validate that claim.

A successful course of action that is valid not only in the Horn of Africa but also around the globe is critical to winning the War on Terror. This is not the only region where a clash of cultures or regional instability exists. In his book, "The Pentagon's New Map" Thomas Barnett describes how he "mapped" a section of the globe to highlight locations for possible military action after September 11, 2001.[58] The area spans the Caribbean Rim, the Andes portion of South America, and the majority of Africa, the Balkans, the Caucasus, central Asia, the Middle East, and Southeast Asia.[59] With resources too limited for another operation on the scale of Iraq or Afghanistan, the U.S. military must have a valid course of action to win the GWOT in these areas. Operations in CJTF-HOA are an example of just such a course of action. The argument will next examine the theory of Information Operations in an operational context.

CHAPTER 2 INFORMATION OPERATIONS – THEORY AND DOCTRINE

Introduction

This anecdote, a description of a typical CJTF-HOA mission, will provide a reference from which to explain the theoretical concept and doctrinal definitions of Information Operations. It is a description of a Medical Civil Action Project (MEDCAP). In this example, a Civil Affairs (CA) team has coordinated for a doctor to travel to a rural village in a country in the Horn of Africa to administer a vaccine to the children of the village and the surrounding area. The doctor arrives and begins administering shots. The doctor vaccinated about 20 children with no negative side effects. The doctor and the CA team thank their hosts and depart for the day.

Over the next week, a story begins to circulate through the village and surrounding area that the vaccination was not to prevent sickness as the Americans promised but instead would sterilize the children. Because of this rumor, when the CA team returned with the doctor for another MEDCAP,

---

[58] Thomas P.M.. Barnett, *The Pentagon's New Map – War and Peace in the Twenty-First Century* (New York: The Berkley Publishing Group, 2005), 154.
[59] Ibid., 149.

no villagers brought their children to the doctor and the ones who had their children vaccinated the last time were angry and almost violent in their demands for a "cure."

Theoretical Definition

This example illustrated the scope of the information environment. Marc J. Romanych provided a basic guide to the information environment and information operations theory in his article "A Theory Based View of IO"

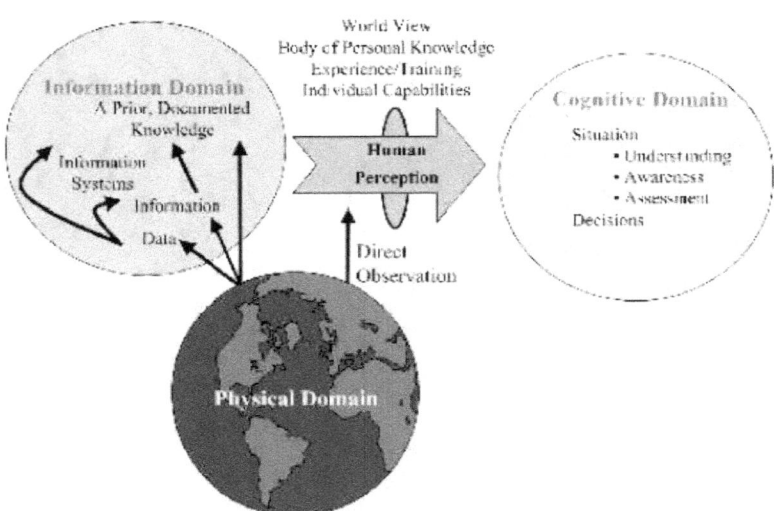

Figure 1 – The Information Environment[60]

In this article, he stated the information environment was an abstract, manufactured construct having three related but distinct domains, Cognitive, Information, and Physical.[61](Fig 1) The physical domain included actions visible to the public, such as a doctor giving a child a vaccination shot. The informational domain was the medium through which the events or actions reached to the audience, the target population. The cognitive domain was the mind of the decision-maker. The decision an individual made or did not make with the information they received, reflected the effect of Information Operations on the information environment.

---

[60]David Alberts, John J. Garstka, Richard E. Hayes, and David A. Signori, *Understanding Information Age Warfare* (Washington, DC: Command and Control Research Program Publication Series, 2001), 11.
[61]Marc Romanych, "A Theory-Based View of IO," *Iosphere*, (Spring 2005) 12.

For example, the action of the doctor vaccinating children in Africa occurred in the physical domain. A news organization or an individual whose aims are contradictory to those of the U.S. could report that action to the villagers. Some villagers and the parents of the children who received the vaccine also directly observed it. The news organization broadcasted the story that a doctor came to the village to help prevent the children from getting sick. An individual who is not supportive of the U.S. mission told the story of an evil woman (the doctor) sticking needles into the arms of children to make them sterile so the population will die. The parents who directly observed the vaccination believed one version or the other based upon the factors influencing their perception identified in Figure 1.

The exaggerated difference between these two reports is possible in areas of Africa. The different possible reports illustrate the point that information will change in the informational domain. The result of this change affects how the decision makers, the parents of the children, perceive that action. The action taken in the physical environment generated a positive or a negative decision based on how they received the information. If the parents believed the first story, about a doctor helping to prevent sickness, when the information reached the cognitive domain, the minds of the parents, they decided to send more children to the doctor the next time. If the parents believed the rumor as in the example, they would not be receptive to future visits.

This example illustrates the importance of synchronization between an action (the physical domain) and the information (through the information domain) to achieve the desired effect in the mind of the decision-maker (the cognitive domain). This is essentially the goal of the U.S. Military operations in CJTF-HOA. Individuals communicate the actions of U.S. and host nation forces to the population. They use radio, television, internet, phone, or face-to-face contact to communicate their message. The mission of information operations was to guide the actions and the information in such a way as to have the desired effect. That is, the decision maker makes a decision favorable to U.S. strategic policy goals in the region whether the decision maker is a head of state or villager. This reinforces the security of the U.S. in view of the GWOT by defeating terrorists' goals and denying terrorists access to recruiting grounds.

Information Operations can also shape the information environment by raising the information threshold to create conditions to facilitate actions U.S. forces want or need to conduct in the physical domain. The information threshold is a concept used to help planners understand and commanders visualize a point at which enemy information-based operations began to undermine friendly forces ability to conduct unconstrained combat operations.[62] Raising the information threshold contributes to achieving information superiority. Information superiority is "an operational advantage derived from having an informational advantage over the opposing force[s]."[63]

The information environment, across Full Spectrum Operations, influences the character of an information operation. Applying the theoretical definition of information operations to civil military or public affairs tasks gives them a mission beyond relaying information or constructing a facility. Tasks conducted as part of an information operation must support goal of informing and influencing the affected population. Everything from the type of task to the way the organization executes the task has an impact on the population. The same is true of combat operations as seen in Al Fajr (Fallujah 2). The purpose of an information operation characterizes it as an information operation. More than the missions or tasks that are part of the operation, the purpose provides the overarching theme. Because this liberal interpretation could confuse responsibilities for planning and executing, doctrine provides a common point of departure for using information operations in a military context.

---

[62] One example of this is the U.S. actions to take Fallujah, Iraq in the fall of 2004. The lessons learned from the spring campaign led U.S. forces to an increased awareness of how enemy information operations could negate successful U.S. combat operations. The planners and commanders coordinated information operations across unit boundaries and across organizations to raise the information threshold. They accomplished this by enhancing coalition information operations and degrading the enemy's access to key terrain needed to conduct their information operations. This created "additional 'maneuver' room for combat operations in Fallujah." The effect of the raised threshold was temporary but significant. Operation Al-Fajr was a maneuver and information operational success. Thomas F. Metz, Mark W. Garrett, James E. Hutton, Timothy W. Bush, Massing Effects in the Information Domain – A Case Study in Aggressive Information Operations, *Military Review* (May-June 2006) 6.

[63] Romanych, 15.

Doctrinal Definitions

At a minimum doctrine provides a common definitions and tasks in a more concrete manner than theory to facilitate the implementation of information operations. The U.S. military conducts Information Operations in support of Full Spectrum operations. In specific campaigns, Information Operations are the Decisive Operation. In areas void of declared hostilities, where the U.S. government is targeting a neutral or friendly population or government, information operations can be effective in denying terrorists the sanctuary and external support they need to survive. It is in this environment information operations can achieve the goals of GWOT. Joint and Army doctrine broadly defined Information Operations as the integrated employment of capabilities to influence an adversary's decision-making. This ability to influence decision-making is a critical piece in winning the GWOT. This relates back to the enemy acknowledging his inability to achieve victory, acknowledging defeat. A more detailed review of the elements of information operations provides a better understanding of this capability.

The specific definition of information operations in JP 3-13 is "The integrated employment of the core capabilities of electronic warfare, computer network operations, psychological operations, military deception, and operations security, in concert with specified supporting and related capabilities, to influence, disrupt, corrupt, or usurp adversarial human and automated decision making while protecting our own." The five supporting capabilities referred to by this definition are information assurance (IA), physical security, physical attack, counterintelligence (CI), and combat camera (COMCAM). The three related capabilities are public affairs (PA), civil military operations (CMO), and defense support to public diplomacy (DSPD).[64]

The distinctions between the capabilities of IO, supporting capabilities of IO and the related capabilities of IO are subtle. The capabilities of IO are the primary means by which the JFC can

---

[64] U.S. Department of Defense, Director for Operations (J-3) *Joint Publication 3-13, Information Operations* (Washington, DC: Joint Staff, 2006), 2-1 Army uses the term element in place of capability, FM 3-13, 2003, 2-1 to 2-28.

influence an adversary and other target audience while enabling friendly forces' freedom of action in the information environment.[65] Referring back to the example of the MEDCAP mission in Africa, few if any elements of IO (EW, CNO, PSYOP, MILDEC, and OPSEC) appear to play a large part. There may be a member of the PSYOP team accompanying the CA team and every mission involves OPSEC to some degree but it is not apparent that the mission required EW, CNO, or MILDEC support.

The supporting capabilities; IA, physical security, physical attack, CI and COMCAM, are either directly or indirectly involved in the information environment, but they also serve other wider purposes.[66] Again referring to the MEDCAP example, a member of the COMCAM would have been on the team to provide quality photos in support of spreading a good news story in the national and international press. Personnel from CI might have been members of the team accompanying the doctor if intelligence reports indicated threat activity in or near the area. The other supporting capabilities most likely played a background role in supporting the higher command.

The related capabilities make significant contributions to IO but IO must not compromise their primary purpose or rules under which they operate.[67] In the case of the MEDCAP example, a CI or PSYOP operation might negate the benefit of the MEDCAP mission and work done by the CA team to gain the trust of the villagers. Unity of effort and the authority and the ability to synchronize the core elements of IO with the related capabilities is vital to achieve the effect of massing IO for the benefit of the overarching mission.

The current Joint and Army publications governing Information Operations offer a common definition of how the U.S. Military applies the theory of Information Operations. Both references refer to a set of core capabilities, supporting capabilities and related capabilities and emphasize that the capabilities must be fully integrated and synchronized to achieve desired results. Planning and

---

[65] U.S. Department of Defense, Director for Operations (J-3) *JP 3-13*, 2-5.
[66] Ibid., 2-8.
[67] U.S. Department of Defense, Director for Operations (J-3), *JP 3-13*, 2-8.

synchronizing these capabilities in current operations have led to a proposed revision in Army doctrine. This revision defines the term Information Engagement.[68]

Proposed Changes

Military doctrine specifically outlines what the elements, the related elements, and the supporting elements of information operations are. The doctrinal definition is so broad that almost any operation could be an information operation. Viewed from this perspective, defining Information Operations is about defining the purpose of the operation more than the elements used in the operation.

This realization has developed slowly beginning with operations in Bosnia and continuing in Africa today. Military commanders have written about recognizing the importance of coordinated information operations to their success. Those lessons include "an emerging recognition among war-fighters that a broader and more aggressive comprehensive and holistic approach to IO-an approach that recognizes the challenges of the global information environment and seamlessly integrates the functions of traditional IO and PA- is required to succeed on the information age battlefield."[69] For combat operations, that meant the Marines had to raise the IO threshold to prevent national or international sentiment from negatively affecting combat operations. For stability operations that means capitalizing on all activities to raise the IO threshold and use positive local and international sentiment to counter enemy operations.

It is with this logic that information operations were determined to be the decisive operation in the course of action chosen by CJTF-HOA. The type of information operations conducted by CJTF-HOA were offensive operations using CMO in support of a PSYOP information campaign and defense support to public diplomacy in the form of mil to mil training events. These operations created the room to "maneuver" so that when other task forces had to come in and conduct direct

---

[68] Hugh Rogers, Lieutenant Colonel, "FM 3-0 Issue Paper: Information Operations (IO)." 5 pages, February 2007, Combined Arms Doctrine Directorate, U.S. Army Combined Arms Center, 4.
[69] Metz et. al., 5.

action type missions, those missions were accepted as necessary by the local population and government.

As the Army finalizes the updated FM 3-0, Operations, this type of information operation task has a new name, Information Engagement. In the current draft of FM 3-0, Information Engagement is the combined use of Public Affairs, Defense Support to Public Diplomacy and Psychological Operations to inform and influence a population, government, or enemy force to effective a positive outcome on friendly operations. In addition to naming this task, the new Army doctrine would no longer characterize civil military operations (CMO) as a related element of IO. [70] Information Engagement would incorporate Civil Military Operations when units planned and conducted them in support of defense support to public diplomacy. This division of the capabilities is based on the type of threat influenced by the capability. For example, the core capability set focused on a peer competitor in an armed conflict. The second set focused on protecting the military from threats during peacetime or a limited conflict. The third set focused on preventing the emergence of a threat by creating and maintaining relations with a possible threat. While this alignment makes sense in a threat-based military, aligning the capabilities along warfighting functions better serves a capability-based military.

Aligning the capabilities of Information Operations along warfighting functions facilitates the synchronization and coordination of Information Operations during planning and execution. [71] This is especially important in an operational command such as CJTF-HOA. The rewrite of FM 3-0 Operations divides Information Operations into five tasks and aligns responsibility for planning and executing these tasks along warfighting functions. The new Army FM 3-0 also assigns staff responsibility for each of the IO tasks. Under this construct, the task of Information Engagement is part of the Command and Control warfighting function and the G-7 has staff responsibility for that

---

[70] Rogers, 3.

[71] The warfighting functions are: intelligence, movement and maneuver, fire support, protection, sustainment, and command and control.

task. The new construct eliminates the need for an Information Operations Working Group. The IO tasks are coordinated and synchronized by the responsible staff sections in the course of executing the Military Decision Making Process of the Joint Operation Planning Process. As the U.S. continues to prosecute this Long War, every improvement in coordination and synchronization will save lives.

Conclusion

The Theory of Information Operations presumes that there is an Information Environment that consists of three domains, Cognitive, Informational, and Physical. Information resides in and travels between these domains. The anecdote of a MEDCAP in CJTF-HOA illustrated how information could change as it traveled between these domains. It also demonstrated that the Information Environment is a complex environment where causal relations are not always apparent. This anecdote underscored the importance of coordination and synchronization to an effective Information Operation. Commanders must understand that this coordination must encompass all warfighting functions.

Joint and Army doctrine provide a common point of departure for how Information Operations align with the warfighting functions. Emerging Army Doctrine would change the current alignment to better facilitate planning and execution of Information Operations. This new doctrinal alignment is extremely relevant to facilitating the replication of CJTF-HOA's success in other regions of the globe.

Current doctrine aligns Information Operations into core, related and supporting capabilities. The core capabilities are electronic warfare (EW), computer network operations (CNO), psychological operations (PSYOP), military deception (MILDEC), and operations security (OPSEC). The supporting capabilities are information assurance (IA), physical security, physical attack, counterintelligence (CI), and combat camera (COMCAM). The three related capabilities are public affairs (PA), civil military operations (CMO), and defense support to public diplomacy (DSPD).[72]

Aligning the capabilities of Information Operations along warfighting functions facilitates the synchronization and coordination of Information Operations during planning and execution.[73] This is especially important in an operational command such as CJTF-HOA. The rewrite of FM 3-0 Operations divides Information Operations into five tasks and aligns responsibility for planning and executing these tasks along warfighting functions. The new Army FM 3-0 also assigns staff responsibility for each of the IO tasks. Under this construct, the task of Information Engagement is part of the Command and Control warfighting function and the G-7 has staff responsibility for that task. The new construct eliminates the need for an Information Operations Working Group. The IO tasks are coordinated and synchronized by the responsible staff sections in the course of executing the Military Decision Making Process of the Joint Operation Planning Process. As the U.S. continues to prosecute this Long War, every improvement in coordination and synchronization will save lives.

CHAPTER 3 THE LONG WAR

Introduction

The success of CJTF-HOA in using information operations is significant for the U.S. military in the context of a Long War. Since the cold War, the United States has not had a significant ideological rival. Within three years of the fall of the Berlin Wall, over half of the countries in the world had a democratic government.[74] To quote Samuel P. Huntington from his book, *The Third Wave: Democratization in the late Twentieth Century* "[democracy is] the only legitimate and viable

---

72 U.S. Department of Defense, Director for Operations (J-3) JP 3-13, 2-1. The Army uses the term element in place of capability, FM 3-13 2003, 2-1 to 2-28.
73 The warfighting functions are: intelligence, movement and maneuver, fire support, protection, sustainment, and command and control.
74Shin, Doh Chull. "On the Third Wave of Democratization: A Synthesis and Evaluation of Recent Theory and Research." World Politics, Vol. 47, No. 1. (Oct 1994), 135.

alternative to an authoritarian regime of any kind."[75] Yet during this same time, the early 90s, members of a fundamental Islamic organization, to include Osama Bin Laden, began to challenge the superiority of western, American style democracy with a call to return to fundamental Islamic rule.

In Chapter seven of the book, *Winning the Long War*, Dr. Cohen highlights a conclusion from Clausewitz *On War* – "that defeat is in the mind of the enemy commander."[76] Although a seemingly obvious lesson of which every military commander is aware, he highlights that this is a much clearer task in a short war as opposed to a long war. An enemy commander in a short war has overwhelming evidence of his defeat; that evidence is far from clear or overwhelming to an enemy commander in a long war. Indeed, because the enemy in a long war, like insurgencies, begins the struggle from a position of weakness defeat must convince him that not only is he weak but that he has no chance to become strong.

A Struggle of Ideas

This is the struggle of ideas described by Dr. Cohen. He lists the key victories in the struggle of ideas as "destroying the legitimacy of a competing ideology, and robbing the enemy of the support of the people."[77] He implies four tasks are critical in achieving these victories. "1) Understanding the enemy; 2) de-legitimizing its view of the world; 3) offering a credible alternative; and 4) demonstrating the will to prevail in the long conflict."[78]

The first step in understanding the enemy is defining who the enemy is. The National Security Strategy (NSS) from 2002 identified our enemy as terrorists, individuals who would execute premeditated, politically motivated violence perpetrated against innocents. The introduction to the 2006 National Security Strategy focused on radical Islamic terrorists as the greatest threat to this

---

[75] Samuel P. Huntington, *The Third Wave, Democracy in the Late Twentieth Century,* Norman: University of Oklahoma Press, 1991, 58.
[76]Carl von Clausewitz, *On War* (New York: Knopf, 1993), 102,103.
[77]Ariel Cohen, "The War of Ideas." in *Winning the Long War : Lessons from the Cold War for Defeating Terrorism and Preserving Freedom.* James J. Carafano and Paul Rosenzweig (Washington, DC: Heritage Foundation, 2005), 174.
[78]Cohen, 174.

nation. It states "Yet a new totalitarian ideology now threatens, an ideology grounded not in secular philosophy but in the perversion of a proud religion. Its content may be different from the ideologies of the last century, but its means are similar: intolerance, murder, terror, enslavement, and repression."[79]

Several groups pose a threat to the U.S. The main groups are the radical Wahhabi/Salafi sects of Sunni Islam in the form of The Muslin Brotherhood, al Qaeda, and Jamaat-I Islami and from Hezbollah, a Shia Islamic sect supported by factions within Iran.[80] The National Islamic Front and the Al Ithaad al Islam (Unity of Islam) are related factions operating in the Horn of Africa.[81] These groups are a threat because they act on their ideology. These groups draw a strict line between themselves and all other Muslims. They target this group of "other Muslims" for conversion to their ideology. If they do not convert, they are killed.[82] They also divide the world into the Land of Islam (Dar al-Islam) and the non-Islamic world known to them as the Land of War (Dar ul-Harb).[83] This other world must be at least subjugated and at best converted.[84] These radical groups will be at war with the western ideology until they achieve their goals.

The goal of these radical Islamic groups is establishment of a Caliphate, governed by Sharia law, over all Islamic lands in its 9th century boundaries and beyond. From this Caliphate, they will engage in jihad to convert the rest of the world to Islam achieving a global Islamic religious government.[85] This goal is in direct competition with the idea of economic and democratic globalization.

To achieve this goal the radical leaders use weapons and words. Western legal systems recognize and prosecute as criminals terrorists who use physical weapons. But these systems are not

---

79 U.S. National Security Council. The National Security Strategy of the United States of America, (Washington, DC: White House, 2006), 1.
80 Cohen, 176.
81 Asefa, 8
82 Cohen, 176.
83 Sherifa Zuhur, "A Hundred Osamas : Islamist Threats and the Future of Counterinsurgency," (Carlisle Barracks: SSI, 2005), 13.
84 Cohen, 179.
85 Cohen, 181.

equipped to stop the "jihad of the tongue."[86] In the Islamic culture, there is not a separation between rhetoric and action; it is a continuum of jihad.[87] Western cultures protect the values of free speech and freedom of religion. With this protection, the radicals are free to initiate their jihad without fear of prosecution. The West began to understand the danger of this threat after September 11.

To defeat the threat from radical Islamists, the U.S. developed a strategy to de-legitimize the Islamists' view of the world. The strategy to defeat terrorists outlined by the 2002 NSS addressed the threat of the enemy's global reach and the need to deny them "what they need to survive: safe haven, financial support, and the support and protection that certain nation-states historically have given them." This NSS also strongly emphasized taking the fight to the enemy before they chose to attack America or her allies again.[88]

In the President's National Strategy for Combating Terrorism (NSCT) published in February of 2003, the broad goals of the 2002 NSS were refined into the 4D strategy, defeat, deny, diminish, and defend. Defeat refers to the goal of defeating the terrorists and their organizations and "calls for defeating terrorist organizations of global reach through the direct or indirect use of diplomatic, economic, information, law enforcement, military, financial, intelligence (MIDLIFE), and other instruments of power." The term deny "stresses denying terrorists the sponsorship, support, and sanctuary that enable them to exist, gain strength, train, plan, and execute their attacks." Diminish "is made up of the collective efforts to diminish conditions that terrorists can exploit." "[Defend] encompasses our nation's collective efforts to defend the United States' sovereignty, territory, and its national interests, at home and abroad." The term defend encompasses the physical protection of the United States, to include its cyber domain, population, property interests and democratic principles.[89] Two other highlights from the 2002 NSS were the requirement for a long-term strategy and the need

---

86Ibid., 182.
87Ibid.
88 U.S. National Security Council. The National Security Strategy of the United States of America, (Washington, DC: White House, 2002), 11.
89 U.S. National Security Council, The National Strategy for Combating Terrorism, (Washington, DC: White House, 2003), 15-24.

to collaborate with friends and allies. This guidance is still in the 2006 NSS. One part of Section Three reads -"In the short run, the fight involves using military force and other instruments of national power to kill or capture the terrorists, deny them safe haven or control of any nation; prevent them from gaining access to WMD; and cut off their sources of support. In the long run, winning the war on terror means winning the battle of ideas, for it is ideas that can turn the disenchanted into murderers willing to kill innocent victims." This statement illustrated the necessity of information operations to the long-term strategy for winning the GWOT.

The 2006 NSS proposed a strategy that would not only defeat the individuals who choose to follow this totalitarian ideology but to prevent its spread to the under governed or ungoverned nations in this world. This mission follows from the statement-

> "In the world today, the fundamental character of regimes matters as much as the distribution of power among them. The goal of our statecraft is to help create a world of democratic, well-governed states that can meet the needs of their citizens and conduct themselves responsibly in the international system. This is the best way to provide enduring security for the American people"[90]

Information Operations in a Struggle of Ideas

The United States must engage this threat, this radical ideology that attacks us every day. Public diplomacy has proven ineffective. More than 80 percent of the Muslim world is strongly anti-American; believe Arabs were not involved in the attack on America September 11, 2001 and that the wars in Afghanistan and Iraq are unjustified.[91] As recently as Jan 2007, Ms. [Karen] Hughes and the State Department are providing minimal support and attention to a Muslim conference where radical reforms, not fundamentalists, are gathering to discuss how to save their religion from the fundamentalists.[92]

Other failures include a lack of capacity to reach beyond traditional diplomacy with the elites and reach the masses to discredit terrorism. The fact that the insurgents have yet to obtain majority

---

[90] U.S. National Security Council. *The National Security Strategy of the United States of America*, (Washington, DC: White House, 2006), Section 1.
[91] Cohen, 183.
[92] Bret Stephens, "Islam's Other Radicals," *The Wall Street Journal*, Tuesday, March 6, 2007, A18.

popular support, even in the most traditional Muslin countries, indicates vulnerability in their ideology. Most nations in the Middle East reserve Sharia law for family disputes and apply western laws to commercial, civil, and criminal situations. Saudi Arabia is the sole exception to this dual legal structure of the Gulf States.[93]

Time to capitalize on this weakness is waning. Wahhabi-directed organizations are rapidly spreading their ideology through youth education. Hundreds of Mosques and Madrassas are springing up throughout Europe, the Middle East and the developing countries, to include the Horn of Africa. These schools are often the only free education available to the poor.[94] They also provide recruiting grounds for the terrorist organizations. The youth are very much a high value target in this war of ideology.[95] One that America and the moderate Muslims must arm with an alternative.[96]

The truth is a part of that arsenal. The " truth about America, the societies of the Greater Middle East and South Asia, including their social problems, their rulers, and the terrorist leaders who prey on them."[97] Our failure to support or develop the voices of traditional, moderate Islam or the progressive liberals in the Islamic world is a problem. Few practicing Muslims do not read classical Arabic and thus rely on the governments and Arab media to provide guidance. The government issues guidance to the muftis, editors and censors who in turn incorporate that guidance into their message that influences the attitude of the "street."[98]

Dr. Cohen broadens his focus on a few other important facts to remember in this GWOT. One is that the majority of the world's Muslims do not live in the Arab countries. Rather Indonesia, Pakistan, and Bangladesh comprise the majority Muslim population centers.[99] In Africa, Ethiopia, Egypt, and Sudan all have larger Muslim populations than Saudi Arabia, Iraq, or Afghanistan. The

---

[93]Cohen, 184.
[94]Cohen, 187.
[95]Cohen, 192.
[96]Authors such as Dr. Sherifa Zuhur assertively defend the idea that there is a moderate Muslim population that the U.S. and Western Nations can work with to reign in radical Islamic Fundamentalists. Sherifa Zuhur, "A Hundred Osamas."
[97]Cohen, 194.
[98]Cohen, 186.
[99]Ibid., 190.

focus cannot be solely on the Middle East. Another is that this war of ideas will require "a long term

investment of wealth and stamina, comparable to that of the Cold War."[100] America must

demonstrate to the world, especially the enemy, a commitment to winning this war. He stresses that

the efforts to win the hearts and minds will require humility and realism, the skills of writers, editors,

linguists, public affairs and area experts.[101]

Achieving Victory in a Struggle of Ideas

The U.S. has not achieved victory through understanding alone. Short-term operations that

de-legitimized the enemy's view of the world and offered a credible alternative are not sufficient in

and of themselves to reach victory. The final task, demonstrate the will to prevail in the long conflict,

is the key to victory in a struggle of ideas.

The U.S. has the resources to fight and win this war. Cost is not the limiting factor. In fact,

the U.S. today is spending less of the GDP on defense than during any other period of war.[102] What

is the limiting factor is the will of the American voter as demonstrated in the 2006 national election.

The way the U.S. fights this war directly influences the will of the American people. Based upon the

Gulf War of 1991, the voters expected a swift and victorious conclusion to liberation of both

Afghanistan and Iraq. The nation needs to sustain the will to see this fight through to victory.

Therefore the chosen course of action must be acceptable not only to the military and civilian

commanders but to the American Public.

In a war such as GWOT, a relevant and useful element of national power for joint military

operations is informational in nature . To some this may sound quite unmilitary but it relates to the

prevention of sanctuary. Authors on counterinsurgency from Galula to Trinquier as well as historians

---

[100]Ibid., 192.
[101]Cohen, 195.
[102] U.S. Office of Management and Budget. " Table 3.1 Outlays by Superfunction and Function 1940-2012." *Historical Tables, Budget of the United States Government, Fiscal Year 2006,*. (2005), 45-52.

Paret and Shy have all written on the value of external support and sanctuary to insurgents[103]. In this global war, it is impossible for the U.S. military to patrol and secure all of the borders around the multiple nations in which terrorists live. Therefore, the US military must influence and empower the governments and populations in those nations to secure their own borders and prevent the rise of terrorism. Combined Joint Task Force – Horn of Africa chose a course of action that emphasized many elements of and related to Information Operations to do just that, inform and influence the population. A course of action in which Information Operations is the decisive operation was adequate, feasible, and acceptable to win the GWOT in regions such as the Horn of Africa.

The United States is not engaged in a fight for land but for ideas. The justification for this change in emphasis is due in a large part to a change in the battlefield; it is social, not geographical. In a war against an enemy whose strength is in their ideology, the key terrain becomes the people. Specifically those individuals who are not in a position to challenge an organization that can control everything they need to survive.

Radical Islamic terrorists are in First and Third World countries alike. With the existence of the world-wide-web and the communication infrastructure in most First World countries, individuals can communicate, train, and receive emotional encouragement to carry out strikes in the virtual world. However, it is in Third World countries that the governments cannot eliminate these conditions with their own institutions and resources. As such, it is in these third world countries, such as those found in the Horn of Africa, where the military, using information operations, can have the greatest effect. The 2006 NSS identifies regional conflicts as a source of instability that negatively affects the national security of the U.S.

> "Regional conflicts are a bitter legacy from previous decades that continue to affect
> our national security interests today. Regional conflicts do not stay isolated for long
> and often spread or devolve into humanitarian tragedy or anarchy. Outside parties
> can exploit them to further other ends, much as al-Qaeda exploited the civil war in
> Afghanistan. This means that even if the United States does not have a direct stake in

---

[103]Thomas A. Bruscino Jr., Out of Bounds, Transnational Sanctuary in Irregular Warfare, Global War on Terror Occasional Paper #17, CSI Press, 81.

a particular conflict, the conflict itself can jeopardize U.S. interests. Outsiders generally cannot impose solutions on parties that are not ready to embrace them, but outsiders can sometimes help create the conditions under which the parties themselves can take effective action"

Some regional conflicts specifically mentioned in the 2006 NSS, Darfur, Uganda, Ethiopia and Eritrea, are located in Africa. Africa is one of the regions in the world where the United States is prosecuting the Global War on Terrorism. To win the GWOT in Africa the U.S. cannot simply repeat its performance in Operation Support Hope - deploy forces when the news media announces a problem and redeploy forces when the press camp departs.

Conclusion

Moreover, this is a Long War. The enemy has been active for the last two generations and there is every indication they will continue in their cause. The U.S. is fighting not just the terrorists themselves but the spread of their ideology. It is a war of ideas, a war for ideals similar to the Cold War. It is for this reason that we must effectively use information operations to win this war. The U.S. must inoculate vulnerable regions against the Radical Islamic ideology to limit its spread. The words and actions of the U.S. and its partners must inform and influence the population to defeat, deny, diminish, and defend their nation against the threat from terrorist organizations and their ideology.

The difficulty in winning such a war is convincing the enemy of his defeat. Dr. Ariel Cohen implied that four tasks were critical in achieving victory in a war of ideas: "1) Understanding the enemy; 2) de-legitimizing its view of the world; 3) offering a credible alternative; and 4) demonstrating the will to prevail in the long conflict."[104] The CJTF-HOA course of action demonstrated that the command understands the enemy. The task force has used Information Operations to accomplish tasks 2 and 3. The key to continued success is to continue mission until the

---

[104]Cohen, 174.

terrorists are convinced of their defeat. Continued presence and action in the Horn of Africa demonstrates that the U.S. has the will to prevail in the long conflict.

CONCLUSION

The sustained presence of Combined Joint Task Force - Horn of Africa in the region is evidence that, at least in this case, the U. S. has learned from its performance in Operation Support Hope. The Soldiers, Sailors, Airmen and Marines can look back on their service and see proof that their efforts at the tactical level resulted in operational and, potentially, strategic victories in the Global War on Terror.

Because of its population, location, and potential resources the Horn of Africa is strategically important to the United States. The region has approximately twenty-five percent of the entire population in Africa and continues to grow. Arab and African Muslims are a significant percent of not just the African population but of the world Muslim population. There are more Muslims in Ethiopia than there are in Saudi Arabia, Iraq, or Afghanistan. This population is key terrain in the Global War on Terror.

The region was important because of its physical terrain as well. The region's location, on the southern border of the historic Caliphate, increased the potential for a Clash of Cultures. This clash was responsible for the difficulty in governing the nations in the region. Nations that had areas that were ungoverned or under-governed attracted terrorist organizations. The terrorists sought sanctuary from the U.S. and other nations fighting the GWOT in these ungoverned or under-governed regions.

These regions provided terrorists with resources in addition to sanctuary. These resources were in the form of money, recruits, or supplies. In the case of Sudan, much of the money came from the oil wealth controlled by the government in the north. CJTF-HOA operations have uncovered terrorist recruits in Kenya and Somalia. The many armed conflicts in the region also provided a steady supply of weapons. This provided the terrorist organizations easy access to large quantities of arms and ammunition. This chaos also made it difficult for the U.S. to prove that nation states outside the region supplied terrorist organizations.

Despite these challenges, CJTF-HOA developed a course of action to win the War on Terror in the Horn of Africa. Because of the mission, resources available to the task force, and the nature of the conflict, the command chose a course of action that used Information Operations as the decisive operation. Specifically they focused on the Information Operation task of Information Engagement to accomplish the mission.

Despite this "soft" approach, CJTF-HOA was not the Peace Corps. Their operations had to accomplish their mission. The course of action that accomplished their mission with the resources available was one in which Information Operations was the decisive operation, specifically the task of Information Engagement. This approach used the resources of the task force to influence the local populations, host nation governments, and international partners to join CJTF-HOA in fighting the Global War on Terror. Subsequent rotations continued with this course of action and have succeeded in winning the Global War on Terror in the Horn of Africa. The accomplishments of CJTF-HOA measured against the U.S. Military Joint Doctrinal criteria validate that claim.

Joint Military doctrine states that a valid COA is one that is adequate, feasible, acceptable, distinguishable, and complete.[105] Since CJTF-HOA already implemented the course of action, the analysis was limited to adequate, feasible, and acceptable. Joint Doctrine defines adequacy as whether the scope and concept of planned operations can accomplish the assigned mission and comply with the planning guidance provided.[106] Army doctrine uses the word suitable but the definitions are similar.[107] Feasibility predicts whether the assigned mission can be accomplished using available resources within the period contemplated by the plan.[108] Acceptability is the

---

[105]U.S. Department of Defense, Director for Operational Plans and Interoperability, *JP 5-0,* III-24.
[106]U.S. Department of Defense, Director for Operational Plans and Interoperability (J-7) *JP 5-0* GL-4.
[107]**Suitable**. A COA must accomplish the mission and comply with the commander's planning guidance. U.S. Army Doctrine Proponency Division, *FM 5-0,* 3-29.
[108]U.S. Department of Defense, Director for Operational Plans and Interoperability (J-7) *JP 5-0* GL-11.

determination as to whether the contemplated course of action is proportional and worth the cost in labor, materiel, and time involved; is consistent with the law of war; and is militarily and politically supportable.[109] CJTF-HOA's performance in the past five years proved that Information Operations were an adequate, feasible, and acceptable course of action to fight the Global War on Terror in the Horn of Africa.

This Information Operations success story begs the question – What are Information Operations? The Theory of Information Operations presumes that there is an Information Environment that consists of three domains, Cognitive, Informational, and Physical. Information resides in and travels between these domains. The anecdote of a MEDCAP in CJTF-HOA illustrated how information could change as it traveled between these domains. It also demonstrated that the Information Environment is a complex environment where causal relations are not always apparent. This anecdote underscored the importance of coordination and synchronization to an effective Information Operation. Commanders must understand that this coordination must encompass all warfighting functions.

Joint and Army doctrine provide a common point of departure for how Information Operations align with the warfighting functions. Proposed Army Doctrine would change the current alignment to better facilitate planning and execution of Information Operations. This new doctrinal alignment is extremely relevant to facilitating the replication of CJTF-HOA's success in other regions of the globe.

Current doctrine aligns Information Operations into core, related and supporting capabilities. The core capabilities are electronic warfare (EW), computer network operations (CNO), psychological operations (PSYOP), military deception (MILDEC), and operations security (OPSEC). The supporting capabilities are information assurance (IA), physical security, physical attack, counterintelligence (CI), and combat camera (COMCAM). The three related capabilities are public

---

[109]U.S. Department of Defense, Director for Operational Plans and Interoperability (J-7) *JP 5-0* GL-4

affairs (PA), civil military operations (CMO), and defense support to public diplomacy (DSPD).[110] This division of the capabilities is based on the type of threat influenced by the capability. For example, the core capability set focused on a peer competitor in an armed conflict. The second set focused on protecting the military from threats during peace time or a limited conflict. The third set focused on preventing the emergence of a threat by creating and maintaining relations with a possible threat. While this alignment makes sense in a threat-based military, aligning the capabilities along warfighting functions better serves a capability-based military.

Aligning the capabilities of Information Operations along warfighting functions facilitates the synchronization and coordination of Information Operations during planning and execution.[111] This is especially important in an operational command such as CJTF-HOA. The rewrite of FM 3-0 Operations divides Information Operations into five tasks and aligns responsibility for planning and executing these tasks along warfighting functions. The new FM 3-0 also assigns staff responsibility for each of the IO tasks. Under this construct, the task of Information Engagement is part of the Command and Control warfighting function and the G-7 has staff responsibility for that task. The new construct eliminates the need for an Information Operations Working Group. The IO tasks are coordinated and synchronized by the responsible staff sections in the course of executing the Military Decision Making Process of the Joint Operation Planning Process. As the U.S. continues to prosecute this Long War, every improvement in coordination and synchronization will save lives.

Moreover, this is a Long War. The enemy has been active for the last two generations and there is every indication they will continue to attack until they acknowledge defeat or achieve their goal of reunifying the Caliphate. This war is a war of ideas, similar to the Cold War. The U.S. is fighting not just the terrorists themselves but the spread of their ideology. It is for this reason that we must effectively use information operations to win this war. The U.S. must inoculate vulnerable

---

[110] U.S. Department of Defense, Director for Operations (J-3) *JP 3-13,* 2-1. The Army uses the term element in place of capability, FM 3-13 2003 pp2-1-2-28.
[111] The warfighting functions are: intelligence, movement and maneuver, fire support, protection, sustainment, and command and control.

regions against the Radical Islamic ideology to limit its spread. The words and actions of the U.S. and its partners must inform and influence the population to defeat, deny, diminish, and defend their nation against the threat from terrorist organizations and their ideology.

The difficulty in winning such a war is convincing the enemy of his defeat. In the book, *Winning the Long War* – Dr. Ariel Cohen implies that four tasks are critical in achieving victory in a war of ideas: "1) Understanding the enemy; 2) de-legitimizing its view of the world; 3) offering a credible alternative; and 4) demonstrating the will to prevail in the long conflict."[112] The key to continued success is for the U.S. to continue the mission until the terrorists are convinced of their defeat. Continued presence and action in the Horn of Africa demonstrates that the U.S. has the will to prevail in the long conflict.

RECOMMENDATIONS

As they are currently structured, Operations in Iraq and Afghanistan are not adequate, feasible, acceptable ways to prosecute the GWOT. Opinion polls and the 2006 elections indicate that the U.S. public is not willing to support the continuation of these operations. This lack of support from the public and Congress may force these operations to conclude before the U.S. achieves the objectives of those operations. Without the support to conduct operations across the globe, the military can only defend the homeland from home, reacting to future terrorist strikes instead of preventing them. The U.S. military must find an adequate, feasible, acceptable course of action in order to continue to receive the necessary support to fight the GWOT. Operations in the Horn of Africa are an example of such a successful course of action.

As the U.S. Military reduces troop commitments in Iraq and Afghanistan, it should apply this course of action to other regions in the globe similar to the Horn of Africa. For the U.S. Military to achieve the maximum benefit of this course of action in new regions, the Military must incorporate the lessons learned from CJTF-HOA. Those lessons cover a range of topics but the most important

---

[112]Cohen, 174.

are command and control, interagency coordination and timeframe. Implementing these lessons learned reduces risk in future operations.

CJTF-HOA learned lessons about command and control (C2) from the time CENTCOM created the task force. Not every service has the option of running a command and control element from the sea until they move into a land-based facility. Future commands must have adequate communication and support in place to accomplish their mission from the start. The truly joint nature of the task force was another lesson for the commands. The C2 structure required staff officers from all services to adequately advise the commander. CJTF-HOA felt these shortages from the perspective of a naval service. Their lack of staff knowledge of the full capabilities of the Army Corps of Engineers delayed their requests for support. The last aspect of the rotations that affected the command and control was personnel rotations. Frequent individual replacements on the staff challenged the command. The average rotation was 90 to 180 days. A section lost approximately two months of productivity with each personnel change. With two or more changes each year, the task force is not operating at peak efficiency.

This rotation also affected the interagency coordination. One of many success stories in CJTF-HOA overcoming their lack of resources was the implementation of the Country Coordination Elements (CCE). These elements greatly enhanced the information flow and decision cycle between the task force and multiple embassies in the region. The frequent personnel rotation also affected the productivity of these cells. The last two CJTF-HOA rotations have increased the number and frequency of interagency and international forums. The task force could have held there events earlier in the rotations if there were less frequent turnover in the personnel coordinating these events. The same is true of the task force's efforts to coordinate their efforts with the NGOs operating in the region. This interaction and coordination is critical to the final recommendation, a realistic timeline for operations such as CJTF-HOA.

The timeline must be generational, twenty to fifty years, and it must include at lease two planned transitions. The first transition is from a predominantly military presence to a predominantly civilian presence. Though CJTF-HOA is supporting the U.S. State Department as the lead agency for the Horn of Africa, the majority of the U.S. government personnel in the region are military. This is necessary now because of the security risks, but there must be a plan, integrated at the operational and strategic levels, for when and how to reduce the military presence. The next transition is from U.S. or U.N. civilians in the lead to host nation civilians in the lead. This is the ultimate goal of the GWOT but it will not happen successfully without a plan. These transitions will take years to accomplish and there will be years between each transition to set the conditions for a successful transition. This reality necessitates a timeline of twenty to fifty years.

This recommendation addresses the concerns of some that the military alone is insufficient to address the root causes of a nation's troubles. America should shift the focus from the military approach to the human security approach," said Guyo Mohamed, director of the Institute of Security Studies, a security research group with offices in South Africa, Kenya, and Ethiopia. "There is a need to alleviate people's suffering on a large scale so that they are not attracted to criminal activities or recruited into terrorist networks." To do this, the United States should be "more engaged in governance issues in the region because some pockets of instability are as a result of people's reaction to bad governance," Mohammed said in an interview. Regional security analysts like David Muchai say the task force has "at least become a deterrent to terrorists" but the stability of Somalia "remains critical to the elimination of terrorism growth in the region." [113]

Implementing these recommendations in future task forces increases their likelihood of success. Implementation may speed results but speed is relative when the timeline is generational. That is one of the benefits of the CJTF-HOA course of action. Information Operations are adequate, feasible, and acceptable for generational operations. This author predicts that future GWOT operations will look more like those in the horn of Africa than either Afghanistan or Iraq.

---

[113] Steve Mbogo, "U.S. Horn of Africa Task Force Steps up Operations." *World Politics Watch – A Foreign Policy and National Security Daily* , 9 August 2006, 1

BIBLIOGRAPHY

Alberts, David S., John J. Garstka, Richard E. Hayes, and David A. Signori. *Understanding Information Age Warfare.* Washington, DC: Command and Control Research Program Publication Series. Database on-line. Available from CCRP, at <http://www.dodccrp.org/files/Alberts_UIAW.pdf. 2001>

Asefa, Sisay. "The Horn of Africa: Background, Scope and Regional Initiatives." *Addis Tribune* 30 May 03 [database on-line], available from Hartford Web Publishing <http://www.hartford-hwp.com/archives/33/025.html>(24 Jan 07)

Barnett, Thomas P.M.. *The Pentagon's New Map – War and Peace in the Twenty-First Century.* New York: The Berkley Publishing Group, 2005.

Bruscino, Thomas A. Jr.. *Global War on Terrorism,* Occasional Paper #17, *Out of Bounds Transnational Sanctuary in Irregular Warfare.* Leavenworth: Combat Studies Institute Press. 2006.

Casey, David P., Lieutenant Colonel, U.S. Marine Corps. Email interview by author, 6 December 2006, Fort Leavenworth. Transcript. Author in possession of transcript, Leavenworth.

von Clausewitz, Carl. *On War.* edited and translated by Michael Howard and Peter Paret. New York: Knopf, 1993.

Cohen, Ariel. "The War of Ideas." in *Winning the Long War : Lessons from the Cold War for Defeating Terrorism and Preserving Freedom.* James J. Carafano and Paul Rosenzweig, 173-197. Washington DC: Heritage Foundation, 2005.

Galula, David. *Counterinsurgency Warfare: Theory and Practice.* St. Petersburg, FL: Hailer Publishing, 2005.

Hamilton, Lee, Thomas H. Kean, and the National Commission on Terrorist Attacks Upon the United States. *The 9/11 Commission Report.* Washington, DC. U.S. G.P.O. 2004.

(FOUO) Hermes, R. D., Jebb, _____ and Hays, _____, *Combined Joint Task Force - Horn of Africa Initial Impressions Report.* Fort Leavenworth: Center for Army Lessons Learned, Assessment Team No. 04-28, [electronic publication] 2004.(FOUO)

Hughes, Karen. "Nominee for Under Secretary for Public Diplomacy and Public Affairs Testimony at confirmation hearing before the Senate Foreign Relations Committee Washington, DC July 22, 2005." The Mission of Public Diplomacy. 2005. at <http://www.state.gov/r/us/2005/49967.htm>. (2 Jan 07)

Huntington, Samuel P. *The Clash of Civilizations and the Remaking of World Order.* New York: Touchstone, 1997.

Huntington, Samuel P. *The Third Wave: Democratization in the Late Twentieth Century.* Norman: University of Oklahoma Press, 1991.

Kaplan, Robert D. *Imperial Grunts: The American Military on the Ground*. New York: Random House, 2005.

Kilpatrick, Terrance G., Major, U.S. Army Reserve. Email interview by author, 18 December 2006, Fort Leavenworth. Transcript. Author in possession of transcript, Leavenworth.

Knight, Darric , Lieutenant Colonel, U.S. Marine Corps. Email interview by author, 4 December 2006, Fort Leavenworth. Transcript. Author in possession of transcript, Leavenworth.

Huddleston, Craig, Colonel, U. S. Marine Corps. "CJTF-HOA SITREP #3" 19 October 2004. Carl Library Electronic Collection. Leavenworth.

Landay, Jonathan S., Shashank Bengali, Mahad Elmi. "U.S. Policy in the Horn of Africa May Aid al-Qaida, Experts Warn." *The Mercury News* 22 Dec 06 [database on-line] (San Jose Mercury News, accessed 2 Jan 07) no longer available on-line.

Mbogo, Steve. "U.S. Horn of Africa Task Force Steps up Operations." *World Politics Watch – A Foreign Policy and National Security Daily* , 9 August 2006. <http://www.worldpoliticswatch.com/article.aspx?id=103> (14 Mar 07)

Metz, Steven. "Learning from Iraq: Counterinsurgency in American Strategy." Monograph for Strategic Studies Institute. Carlisle Barracks, PA, 2007. [database on-line] (Strategic Studies Institute, accessed 29 Mar 07), available at http://www.strategicstudiesinstitute.army.mil/pubs/display.cfm?pubID=752

Metz, Thomas F., Mark W. Garrett, James E. Hutton, Timothy W. Bush. "Massing Effects in the Information Domain – A Case Study in Aggressive Information Operations." *Military Review* (May/June 2006) 2-12.

Nagl, John A. *Learning to Eat Soup With a Knife : Counterinsurgency Lessons from Malaya and Vietnam*. Chicago: University of Chicago Press, 2005.

Jenkins, Brian Michael, Gregory F. Treverton. "Misjudging The Jihad: Briefing Osama on All the War's Wins and Losses." *San Francisco Chronicle*, November 13, 2005. at <http://www.rand.org/commentary/111305SFC.html>(30 Mar 07)

Office of the Assistant Secretary of Defense (Public Affairs). "News Briefing with Maj. Gen. Timothy Ghormley." U. S. Department of Defense . 21 September 2005. at <http://www.defenselink.mil/transcripts/2005/tr20050921-3962.html> (14 Mar 07)

O'Neill, Bard E. *Insurgency & Terrorism : From Revolution to Apocalypse*. Washington, D.C.: Potomac Books, 2005.

Power, Samantha. *A Problem from Hell : America and the Age of Genocide*. New York: Perennial, 2003.

Prendergast, John, Colin Thomas-Jensen. "Blowing the Horn." *Foreign Affairs* Vol 86, No. 2 (March/April 2007): 59-74.

Romanych, Marc. "A Theory-Based View of IO." *Iosphere* (Spring 2005):12-16

Public Affairs Office, Camp Lemonier Djibouti. "Kenya, Tanzania, Uganda and U.S. to Conduct Multi-Lateral Exercise: Humanitarian Projects Also Scheduled in all EAC Nations During Exercise NATURAL FIRE 2006." CJTF-HOA - Public Website. 3 August 2006. at <http://www.hoa.centcom.mil/Stories/Aug06/20060803-003.htm> (25 January 2007)

Rogers, Hugh, Lieutenant Colonel. "FM 3-0 Issue Paper: Information Operations (IO)." 5 pages, February 2007. Combined Arms Doctrine Directorate, U.S. Army Combined Arms Center. Copy given to the author 2 March 2007.

Sageman, Marc. *Understanding Terror Networks*. Philadelphia: University of Pennsylvania Press, 2004.

Stephens, Bret, "Islam's Other Radicals." *The Wall Street Journal* (Tuesday, March 6, 2007) A18.

Trinquier, Roger. *Modern Warfare: A French View of Counterinsurgency*. New York: Praeger, 1964.

Turabian, Kate L. *A Manual for Writers of Term Papers, Theses, and Dissertations*. 6th ed. rev. by John Grossman and Alice Bennett. Chicago: University of Chicago Press, 1996.

U.S. Army Doctrine Proponency Division, *Field Manual 5-0, Army Planning and Orders Production*. Fort Leavenworth. US Army Combined Arms Center. [electronic publication] Database on-line. Available from Army Publishing Directorate, 2005.

U.S. Army Doctrine Proponency Division, *Field Manual 3-13, Information Operations: Doctrine, Tactics, Techniques, and Procedures*. Washington, DC. Headquarters, Department of the Army. [electronic publication] Database on-line. Available from Army Publishing Directorate, 2003.

U.S. Central Intelligence Agency. "Ethiopia." *The World Factbook*, 15 March 2007. at <https://www.cia.gov/cia/publications/factbook/geos/et.html#People> (28 Mar 07)

U.S. Central Intelligence Agency. "Saudi Arabia." *The World Factbook*, 15 March 2007. at <https://www.cia.gov/cia/publications/factbook/geos/sa.html#People> (28 Mar 07)

U.S. Central Intelligence Agency. "Afghanistan." *The World Factbook*, 15 March 2007. at <https://www.cia.gov/cia/publications/factbook/geos/af.html#People> (28 Mar 07)

U.S. Central Intelligence Agency. "Iraq." *The World Factbook*, 15 March 2007. at <https://www.cia.gov/cia/publications/factbook/geos/iz.html#People> (28 Mar 07)

U.S. Central Intelligence Agency. "Sudan." *The World Factbook*, 15 March 2007. at <https://www.cia.gov/cia/publications/factbook/geos/su.html#People> (28 Mar 07)

U.S. Central Intelligence Agency. "Egypt." *The World Factbook*, 15 March 2007. at <https://www.cia.gov/cia/publications/factbook/geos/eg.html#People> (28 Mar 07)

U.S. Department of Defense. CJTF-HOA, Public Affairs Office. "CJTF-HOA Fact Sheet." CJTF-HOA - Public Website. December 2006. at <http://www.hoa.centcom.mil/facts.htm> (2 Jan 07)

U.S. Department of Defense, Director for Operations (J-3) Joint Publication 3-13, *Information Operations*. Washington, DC: Joint Staff. [electronic publication] Database on-line. Available from CJCS JEL, DTIC, 2006

U.S. Department of Defense, Director for Operational Plans and Interoperability (J-7) *Joint Publication 5-0, Joint Operation Planning*. Washington, DC: Joint Staff. [electronic publication] Database on-line. Available from CJCS JEL, DTIC, 2006.

U.S. Department of Defense, Director for Operations (J-3) *Joint Publication 3-0, Joint Operations*. Washington, DC: Joint Staff. [electronic publication] Database on-line. Available from CJCS JEL, DTIC, 2006.

U.S. Department of Energy. "Country Analysis Briefs- Horn of Africa." Energy Information Administration, USG. February 2006. at <http://www.eia.doe.gov/emeu/cabs/Horn_of_Africa/pdf.pdf> (1 Apr 07)

U.S. National Security Council. *The National Security Strategy of the United States of America*. U.S. National Security Council. Washington, DC, 2002. [electronic publication] available at <http://www.whitehouse.gov/nsc/nss/2002>(14 Dec 06)

U.S. National Security Council. *The National Security Strategy of the United States of America*. U.S. National Security Council. Washington, DC, 2006. [electronic publication] available at <http://www.whitehouse.gov/nsc/nss/2006>(14 Dec 06)

U.S. National Security Council. *The National Strategy for Combating Terrorism* (Feb 2003), U.S. National Security Council. Washington, DC, 2003. [electronic publication] (White House Server, accessed 14 Dec 06) no longer available on-line.

U.S. National Security Council. *The National Strategy for Combating Terrorism* (Sep 2006), U.S. National Security Council. Washington, DC, 2006. [electronic publication] available at <http://www.whitehouse.gov/nsc/nsct/2006/nsct2006.pdf>(29 Mar 07)

U.S. Office of Management and Budget. " Table 3.1 Outlays by Superfunction and Function 1940-2012." *Historical Tables*, Budget of the United States Government, Fiscal Year 2006. 2005. at <http://www.whitehouse.gov/omb/budget/fy2006/pdf/hist.pdf> (13 Feb 07)

Warren, Paul, Lieutenant Colonel, U.S. Army. Email interview by author, 24 October 2006, Fort Leavenworth. Transcript. Author in possession of transcript, Leavenworth.

Westover, David. "Host nation coordinators conference big success at combined joint task force - horn of Africa" CJTF-HOA - Public Website. 10 June 2006. at <http://www.hoa.centcom.mil/Stories/Jun06/20060610-001.htm> (25 Jan 07)

Zuhur, Sherifa. "A Hundred Osamas : Islamist Threats and the Future of Counterinsurgency." Monograph for Strategic Studies Institute. Carlisle Barracks, PA, 2005. [database on-line] available at <http://www.strategicstudiesinstitute.army.mil/pubs/display.cfm?pubID=636> (29 Mar 07)

Shinn, David. "Fighting Terrorism in East Africa and the Horn." *Foreign Service Journal* (September 2004) 36-42

Shin, Doh Chull. "On the Third Wave of Democratization: A Synthesis and Evaluation of Recent Theory and Research." *World Politics,* Vol. 47, No. 1. (Oct 1994), pp135-170. available at <http://links.jstor.org/sici?sici=0043-8871%28199410%2947%3A1%3C135%3AOTTWOD%3E2.0.CO%3B2-M>(30 Mar 07)

APPENDIX A - Map of CJTF-HOA Joint Operations Area[114]

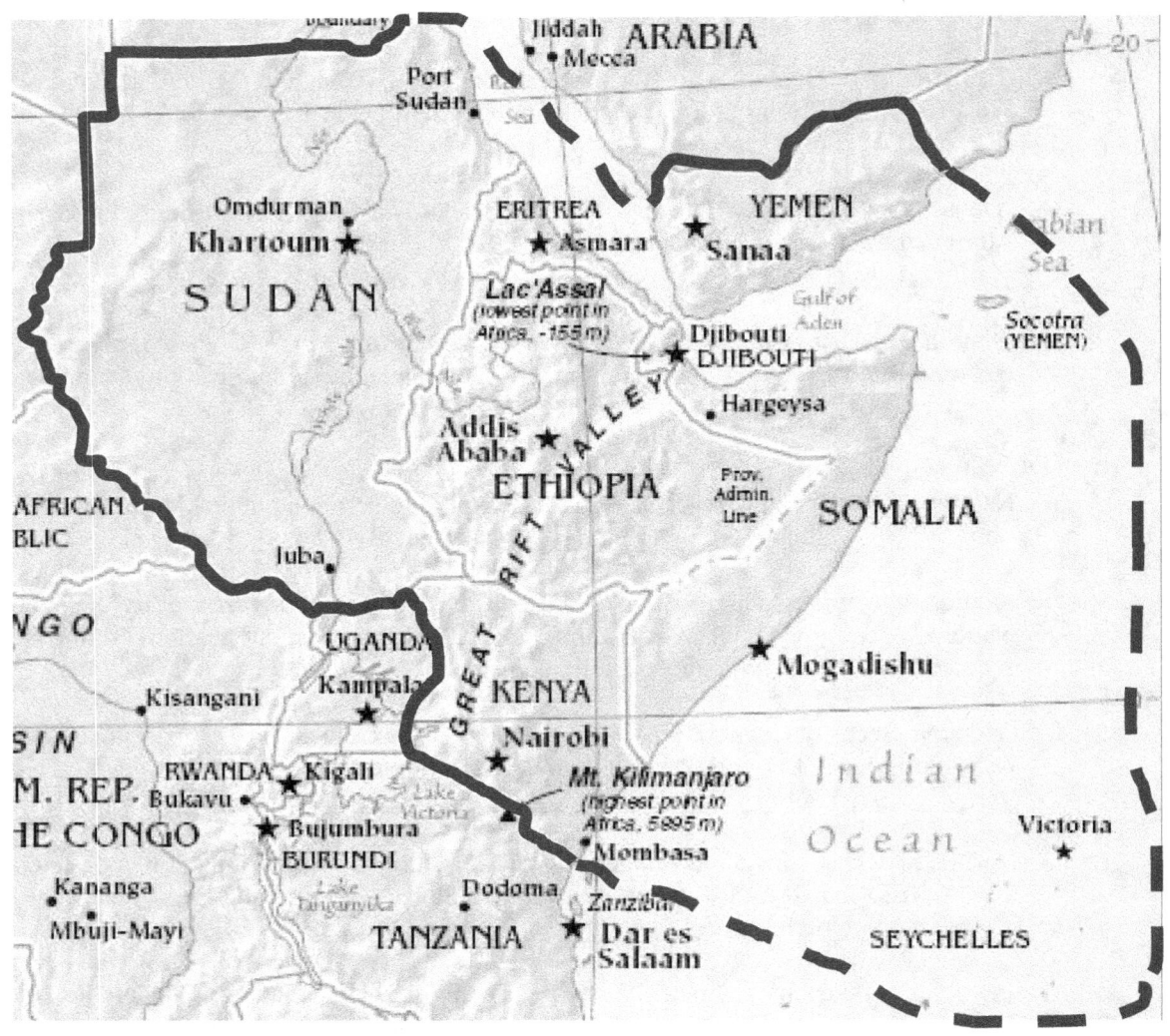

---

[114] Map copied from CIA, *The World Factbook*, AOR boundary drawn by author to include the countries listed in the CJTF-HOA Fact Sheet. This is not to be interpreted as a mission boundary.

APPENDIX B - Table of Proposed Army IO Tasks and Alignment

IO TASKS	CELL/SECTION	IO CAPABILITIES
Military Deception	Plans	Military Deception
Operations Security	Protection	Operational Security
Command and Control Warfare	Fire Support	Electronic Attack Electronic Warfare Support
Information Protection	C4OPS	Information Assurance Computer Network Defense
Information Engagement	IECOORD	Public Affairs Psychological Operations Combat Camera -------------------------------- Coordinated w/ CA and DSPD

Plans is part of Movement and Maneuver

C4OPS is part of Command and Control

IECOORD is part of Command and Control